Wet Deposition Monitoring Protocol
Monitoring Atmospheric Pollutants in Wet Deposition

Natural Resource Report NPS/NRPC/ARD/NRTR—004

Ellen Porter and Kristi Morris
National Park Service, Air Resources Division
WASO-ARD
P.O. Box 25287
Denver, CO 80225-0287

April 2007

U.S. Department of the Interior
National Park Service
Air Resources Division
Denver, Colorado

The Natural Resource Publication series addresses natural resource topics that are of interest and applicability to a broad readership in the National Park Service and to others in the management of natural resources, including the scientific community, the public, and the NPS conservation and environmental constituencies. Manuscripts are peer-reviewed to ensure that the information is scientifically credible, technically accurate, appropriately written for the intended audience, and is designed and published in a professional manner.

The Natural Resources Technical Reports series is used to disseminate the peer-reviewed results of scientific studies in the physical, biological, and social sciences for both the advancement of science and the achievement of the National Park Service's mission. The reports provide contributors with a forum for displaying comprehensive data that are often deleted from journals because of page limitations. Current examples of such reports include the results of research that addresses natural resource management issues; natural resource inventory and monitoring activities; resource assessment reports; scientific literature reviews; and peer reviewed proceedings of technical workshops, conferences, or symposia.

Views and conclusions in this report are those of the authors and do not necessarily reflect policies of the National Park Service. Mention of trade names or commercial products does not constitute endorsement or recommendation for use by the National Park Service.

This report was originally written and distributed in August 2005, but was reformatted and published in the Natural Resources Technical Reports series in April 2007 under the new National Park Service report standards. This report is available from the Air Resources Division website (http://www2.nature.nps.gov/air/) on the internet.

Please cite this publication as:

Porter, E., Morris, K. 2007. Wet Deposition Monitoring Protocol: Monitoring Atmospheric Pollutants in Wet Deposition. Natural Resource Technical Report NPS/NRPC/ARD/NRTR—004. National Park Service, Fort Colins, Colorado.

NPS D-1655, April 2007

Contents

1.0 OVERVIEW

1.1 BACKGROUND

Atmospheric deposition is the process by which airborne particles and gases are deposited to the earth's surface either through precipitation (rain, snow, clouds, and fog) or as a result of complex atmospheric processes such as settling, impaction, and adsorption, known as dry deposition. Deposition can include a wide variety of natural and anthropogenic pollutants, including inorganic elements and compounds (e.g., nitrogen, sulfur, basic cations, mercury and other metals) and organic compounds (e.g., pesticides and herbicides). Once deposited, pollutants can have a variety of ecosystem effects. Nitrogen and sulfur compounds, for example, can result in acidification of freshwaters, loss of aquatic species, eutrophication of estuarine and near-coastal waterways, soil nutrient and base cation leaching, and vegetation changes.

The National Park Service (NPS) is responsible for the protection and conservation of the areas it manages in order to "leave them unimpaired for the enjoyment of future generations" (Organic Act of 1916). NPS also has an affirmative responsibility under the Clean Air Act to protect parks and their resources from sources of air pollution and to participate in national and regional initiatives to control air pollution. Protecting resources in our national parks from air pollution requires extensive knowledge about the origin, transport, and transformation of pollutants and the ecological effects that may result.

Since the late 1970s, the NPS Air Resources Division (ARD) has managed a comprehensive air quality program, emphasizing the collection of credible air quality information to support scientifically sound resource management decisions in parks. In general, air quality monitoring in parks, including monitoring of atmospheric deposition, ozone, and visibility, is done in conjunction with national networks. Information on NPS air quality monitoring and access to data is available at http://www2.nature.nps.gov/air/monitoring/index.htm. Cooperation between NPS and the national air quality monitoring networks has been successful in producing high quality, defensible data that are spatially and temporally comparable, and provides a broad context for an individual park's air quality data. It is strongly recommended that resource managers considering long-term air quality monitoring adopt this cooperative approach, because partnerships with national monitoring networks use limited funding more effectively and provide a more complete database on which to base air quality management decisions. Certain resource management and research questions may be answered by short-term or episodic monitoring with methods outside the scope of this protocol. Such air quality monitoring and research activities by agency and university scientists should be encouraged to gain a better understanding of ecosystems and how they might be affected by air pollution.

Table 1-1 lists the three nationwide networks that monitor atmospheric deposition in the U.S.

Table 1-1

Atmospheric Deposition Monitoring Networks

Network	Measured Parameters	Information and Data
National Atmospheric Deposition Program/National Trends Network (NADP/NTN)	Wet deposition of sulfate, nitrate, ammonium, calcium, magnesium, potassium, sodium, chloride; pH, acidity	http://nadp.sws.uiuc.edu/
National Atmospheric Deposition Program/Mercury Deposition Network (MDN)	Wet deposition of mercury	http://nadp.sws.uiuc.edu/mdn/
Clean Air Status and Trends Network (CASTNet)	Dry deposition of sulfate, nitrate, ammonium, nitric acid, sulfur dioxide	http://www.epa.gov/castnet/

Figure 1-1 shows the locations of deposition samplers on NPS lands.

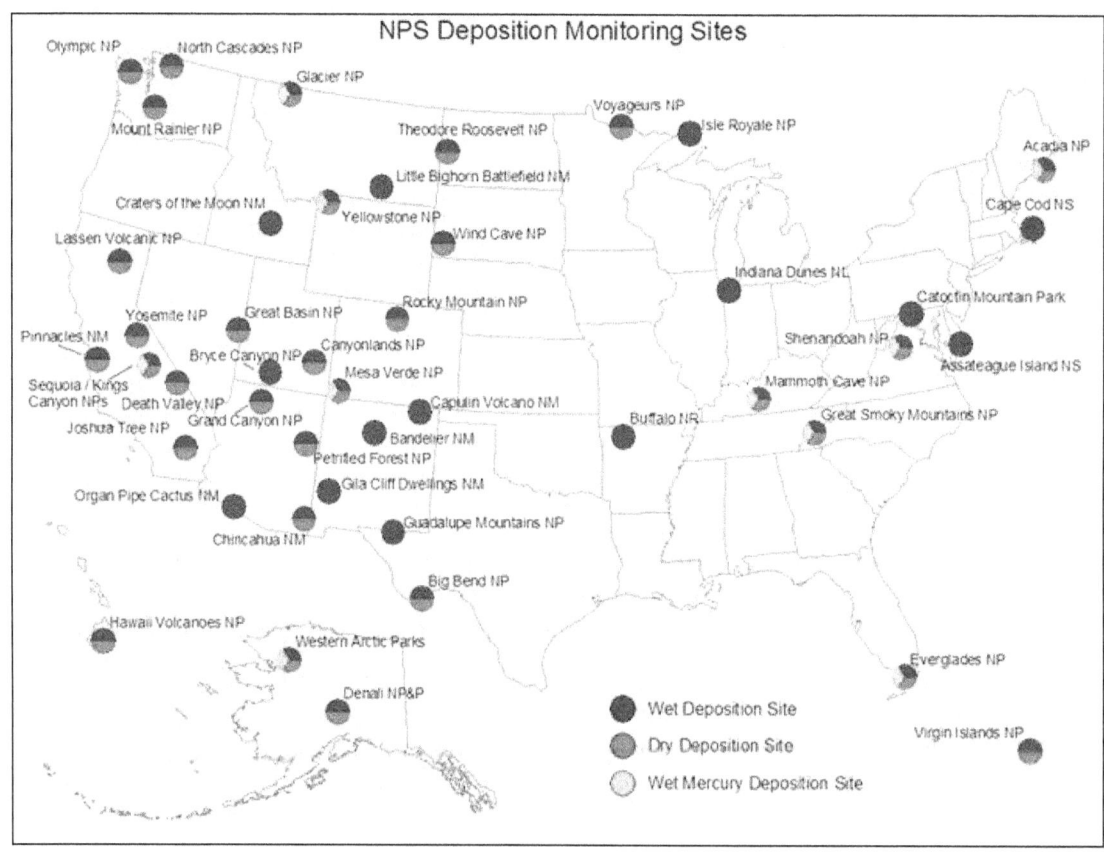

Figure 1-1. NPS monitoring sites for wet, dry, and wet mercury deposition (from http://www2.nature.nps.gov/air/monitoring/deplist.cfm).

This protocol addresses monitoring of wet deposition under the NADP/NTN. The Mercury Deposition Network (MDN) and the Clean Air Status and Trends Network (CASTNet) are covered in separate protocols.

NADP/NDN began operation in 1978 and currently consists of over 240 stations nationwide. Samples are collected using a standardized protocol and are analyzed in a central laboratory using uniform techniques and procedures. The network provides information based on weekly precipitation samples that are analyzed for several chemical constituents, such as acidity (pH), sulfate, nitrate, ammonium, and calcium. Data are presented in terms of concentration and deposition. Concentration data, expressed in milligrams per liter (mg/L) of precipitation are useful in determining spatial and temporal trends because they are not dependent on the amount of precipitation at each site, which can vary substantially from year to year. Wet deposition, expressed in kilograms per hectare per year (kg/ha/yr) is calculated by taking into account both the amount of precipitation and the concentration at each location. Years with higher amounts of precipitation will yield higher levels of wet deposition. Wet deposition data provide the total amount of pollutants actually deposited on the ground by rain and snow and quantify the pollutant input to ecosystems.

In areas with large amounts of clouds and fog or snow, the NADP/NTN bucket may underestimate wet deposition. The NADP/NTN bucket is not designed to collect cloud and fog deposition or blowing snow, and may be overwhelmed by large snow events. Specialized methods for measuring deposition from clouds and fog have been used on a limited site-specific basis. For example, the Environmental Protection Agency's (EPA) Mountain Acid Deposition Program (MADPro) has measured deposition from clouds and fog at three sites in the eastern U.S., including Great Smoky Mountains National Park (NP) (http://www.publica.fhg.de/documents/B-61687.html). Deposition in high-elevation, high snowfall areas, including the Rocky Mountains, has been sampled by digging snowpits (http://water.usgs.gov/pubs/of/2001/ofr01-466/).

1.2 EFFECTS OF ATMOSPHERIC DEPOSITION OF NITROGEN AND SULFUR COMPOUNDS

Nitrogen and sulfur compounds are emitted by a variety of both anthropogenic and natural sources, including automobiles, power plants, industries, agriculture, and fires. Combined with moisture, nitrates and sulfates become acidic and deposit as "acid rain." Acid deposition affects freshwater lakes, streams, and watersheds. Effects include changes in water chemistry that affect algae, fish, submerged vegetation, and amphibian and aquatic invertebrate communities. These changes can result in higher food chain impacts in park ecosystems. Deposition can also cause chemical changes in soils that affect soil microorganisms, plants, and trees. In addition to acidification effects, deposition of nitrogen compounds may cause fertilization or eutrophication. Nitrogen fertilization of natural ecosystems is usually undesirable and can favor certain species of plants over others, altering plant communities and facilitating invasion of non-native species. Excess nitrogen also contributes to nutrient enrichment in coastal and estuarine ecosystems, the symptoms of which include toxic algal blooms, fish kills, and loss of plant and animal diversity.

High elevation ecosystems in the Rocky Mountains, Cascades, Sierra Nevada, southern California, and the upland areas of the eastern U.S. are generally the most sensitive to the acidifying effects of deposition due to their poor ability to neutralize acid deposition. Streams in both Shenandoah and Great Smoky Mountains NPs are experiencing chronic and episodic acidification that has affected brook trout fisheries. Other potentially sensitive areas include the upper Midwest and New England. In addition, many ecosystems are sensitive to the enrichment effects of nitrogen deposition, including those with short growing seasons (i.e., a limited capacity to use available nitrogen) and those that have evolved under low nutrient conditions. Nitrogen sensitive areas include high-elevation ecosystems, arid ecosystems, grasslands, and shallow bays and estuaries along the Atlantic and Gulf Coasts. Changes in aquatic and terrestrial ecosystems attributable to nitrogen deposition have been documented in Rocky Mountain NP and studies are underway at other parks to evaluate nitrogen effects. For more information see *Air Quality in the National Parks*, 2nd edition, at http://www2.nature.nps.gov/air/pubs/aqnps.htm).

1.3 RESOURCE MANAGEMENT OBJECTIVES

Resource managers may want to initiate on-site wet deposition monitoring to assess risks to sensitive lakes, streams, soils and vegetation within their park unit. Managers should first consider whether representative monitoring data are currently available. Figure 1-1, maps available on the NADP/NTN web site (http://nadp.sws.uiuc.edu/), and NPS Air Atlas (http://www2.nature.nps.gov/air/Maps/AirAtlas/index.htm) will help identify existing monitors. NPS has wet deposition samplers in 47 parks that are part of the NADP/NTN network. The majority of parks, however, have no on-site or nearby monitoring. Deposition estimates for these parks are available on NPS Air Atlas (http://www2.nature.nps.gov/air/Maps/AirAtlas/index.htm). These estimates may or may not be representative depending on distance to the monitors used for the estimates, geography, meteorology, and topography. Even for parks with on-site monitoring, a single monitor in a park may not be representative of the entire park if the park is large or has significant variation in elevation and meteorology. Resource managers are encouraged to contact ARD for technical guidance and assistance in developing any monitoring plans.

Atmospheric deposition of nitrogen and sulfur is not regulated under the Clean Air Act. However, data from NADP/NTN are used by the EPA to assess progress in achieving emissions reductions of nitrogen oxides and sulfur dioxide under the Act. NPS uses NADP/NTN data to track progress towards goals established under the Government Performance and Reporting Act for sulfate and nitrate concentrations in precipitation in parks (http://www2.nature.nps.gov/air/who/GPRA/GPRA2004review02042005.pdf).

ARD is developing strategies for estimating the amount of deposition that causes harm to ecosystems. This "critical load" is defined as the amount of pollutant deposition below which significant harmful effects to sensitive resources do not occur. Deposition monitoring and research on ecosystem effects will facilitate the identification of critical loads for park resources. A target load is often used in conjunction with a critical load and is the amount of pollutant deposition that will result in an acceptable level of resource protection, taking into account political, economic, or temporal considerations. For NPS lands, target loads will be selected that are lower than critical loads, to provide a conservative level of protection. Deposition monitoring will enable managers to evaluate whether deposition is below or above critical or target loads.

Atmospheric deposition estimates are also used by NPS ARD in reviewing permit applications for proposed new sources of air pollution (e.g., power plants) near parks. Proponents of new sources are required to analyze their contribution to existing deposition and compare that contribution to thresholds developed by ARD. These deposition analysis thresholds, described at http://www2.nature.nps.gov/air/Permits/flag/NSDATGuidance.htm, are based on estimates of natural background nitrogen and sulfur deposition.

Natural background deposition of nitrogen or sulfur for the East = 0.50 kg/ha/yr
Natural background deposition of nitrogen or sulfur for the West = 0.25 kg/ha/yr

The deposition analysis thresholds are fractions of natural background (0.01 kg/ha/yr for either nitrogen or sulfur in the East; 0.005 kg/ha/yr for either nitrogen or sulfur in the West) because it is assumed that over time, a number of new sources could be adding to deposition. This approach is intended to balance reasonable development and growth with park ecosystem protection. If a proposed source's contribution to deposition is less than the applicable deposition analysis threshold, the contribution is considered insignificant. If the proposed source's contribution exceeds the threshold, and existing deposition is above the critical load for a park, the contribution is considered significant and the source will be asked to mitigate impacts by reducing emissions.

In order to most accurately estimate total deposition, both wet and dry deposition measurements are required (as noted above, cloud, fog, and snow measurements may also be important in some areas). Dry deposition monitoring sites are comparatively few in number; therefore, in areas where only wet deposition is measured, total deposition is often estimated by doubling wet deposition. Figures 1-2 and 1-3 illustrate the proportion of wet to dry deposition in total nitrogen and sulfur deposition at 51 sites for 2001. Doubling wet deposition to estimate total deposition may overestimate in some cases, underestimate in others, but is often our best estimate. The figures also indicate that deposition in all areas exceeds natural background estimates.

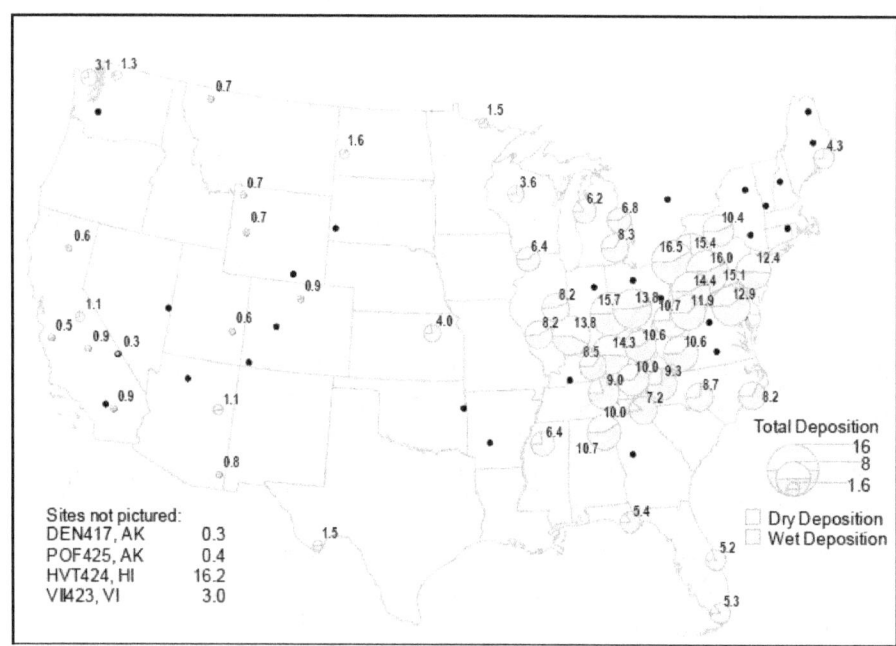

Figure 1-2. Scaled pie charts depict the 2003 total sulfur deposition in kilograms per hectare at 51 CASTNet sites. Wet deposition data (blue) are from NTN sulfate measurements. Dry deposition data (yellow) are from CASTNet sulfur dioxide and sulfate measurements. Total sulfur deposition is indicated in or next to each pie chart.

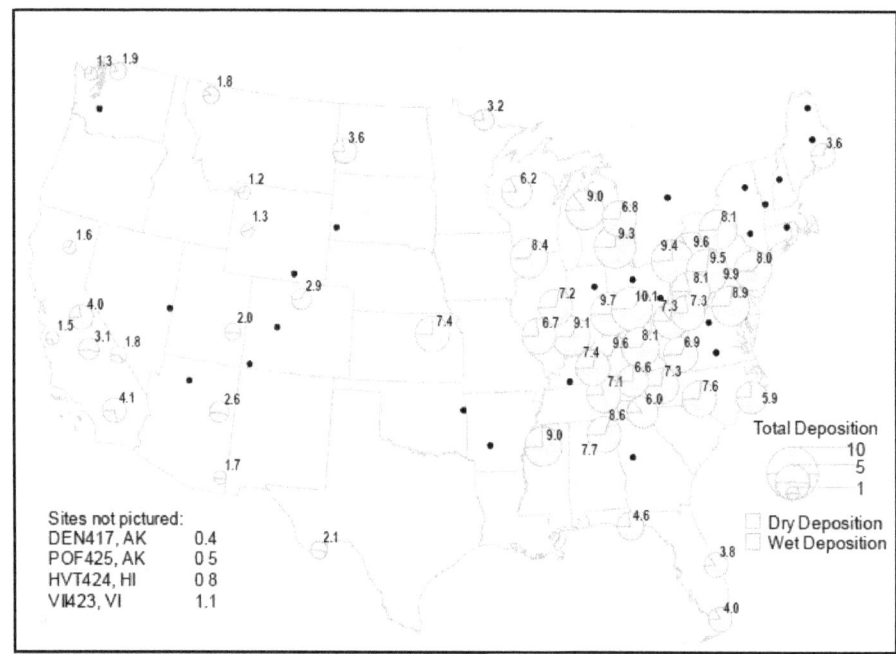

Figure 1-3. Scaled pie charts depict the 2003 total nitrogen deposition in kilograms per hectare at 51 CASTNet sites. Wet deposition data (blue) are from NTN nitrate and ammonium measurements. Dry deposition data (yellow) are from CASTNet nitric acid, nitrate, and ammonium measurements. Total nitrogen deposition is indicated in or next to each pie chart.

6

2.0 WET DEPOSITION MONITORING

2.1 SAMPLING DESIGN

Table 2-1 summarizes operating requirements for an NADP/NTN site (detailed costs are given in Table 2-2).

Table 2-1

Wet Deposition NTN Monitoring Requirements Summary

Data	Siting Criteria	Utilities Required	Shelter Required	Operator Weekly Effort[1]	Typical Initial Cost[2]	Typical Annual Cost[3]
Weekly	Rigid	AC or Solar	No	<1 hour	$17,531	$6,361
[1]Excluding travel time to/from the monitoring site.				[3]Excluding site operator labor costs.		
[2]Including capital costs and installation.						

NADP uses a standard precipitation collector at all its sites. Either line power or solar power is needed to operate the collector. An electronic moisture sensor causes the lid to retract from the sample bucket, allowing a precipitation sample to be collected. Every week on Tuesday mornings, operators all over the country retrieve the samples, weigh them, transfer the sample to a shipping bottle and send it to the NADP Central Analytical Laboratory in Champaign, Illinois. Each site is also equipped with a raingage to record precipitation amounts.

Figure 2-1. NADP/NTN Sampler

Information on NADP/NTN is at http://nadp.sws.uiuc.edu. This web site contains a monitoring site selection and installation manual, a site operation manual, and quality management and quality assurance plans. Site data are also available on the web site, including annual, seasonal, monthly, and weekly data, and trend plots. NADP/NTN ensures the collection of high quality data at its monitoring sites. The network: 1) designates specific precipitation collection equipment to be used throughout the network which allows precipitation to be recorded, collected, and verified; 2) requires this equipment to be maintained in good working order at the original approved location; 3) specifies a strict weekly sampling protocol and a clear definition of sample types; 4) requires every sample to be analyzed at a single laboratory, the Central Analytical Laboratory operated by the Illinois State Water Survey, Champaign, Illinois; and 5) expects each site to operate continuously for a 5-10 year period.

The *NTN (NADP) Site Selection and Installation Manual* (http://nadp.sws.uiuc.edu/lib/manuals/siteinst.pdf) contains information on sampling strategy, and site selection, installation, and testing. Siting criteria include regional, local, and on-site requirements for the raingage and precipitation collector. It lists requirements for the sponsoring agency (e.g., NPS) and the site operator (e.g., NPS employee or contractor), who is responsible for the monitoring equipment, site maintenance, and sample collection. The manual also discusses power requirements and facilities and equipment for measurements of field pH and conductivity. Measurements of field pH and conductivity are no longer required, as of January 2005. Lastly, the manual discusses site installation and testing.

2.2 FIELD METHODS

In general, every Tuesday morning at 0900 local time the site operator changes the sample collection bucket, checks the raingage and replaces the rainfall recording chart, completes a field observer report form, weighs and packages the sample, and mails the sample to the NADP Central Analytical Laboratory. These procedures take approximately 30-60 minutes, which does not include travel time to the site. The *NTN (NADP) Site Operation Manual* (http://nadp.sws.uiuc.edu/lib/manuals/opman.pdf) discusses the site operating procedure, site maintenance, quality assurance procedures, and equipment troubleshooting. It also describes in detail the responsibilities of the site operator and the site supervisor.

2.3 DATA HANDLING AND ANALYSIS

The *NTN (NADP) Quality Management Plan* (http://nadp.sws.uiuc.edu/lib/qaplans/NADP-QMP-Dec2003.pdf) describes the NADP organization, quality management activities, policies, and procedures. It describes planning, documents and records, personnel qualification and training, and computer software and hardware. A specific quality assurance plan for the NTN is available upon request from NADP (http://nadp.sws.uiuc.edu/).

The *Central Analytical Laboratory (CAL) Quality Assurance Plan* (http://nadp.sws.uiuc.edu/lib/qaplans/qapCal2002.pdf) describes the operations of the analytical laboratory, including sample and data processing. It describes data retrievals, procedures, and programs that summarize, check, screen, edit, and report data.

2.4 MONITORING COSTS

Monitoring costs are described in detail in Table 2-2.

Table 2-2
November 2004 Monitoring Costs for Wet Deposition NTN Monitoring

		Costs
Initial/Start-up		
Equipment	• NADP Precipitation Collector with trickle charger (includes shipping)[1]	$2,300
	• 12-volt automotive battery, 300-500 CCA	$70
	• Belfort Universal Recording Rain Gauge #B-5-7802[2] with 12" chart, NADP event marker[3] & 192-hour gear cluster	$3,600
	• Analytical Balance	$1000
	• Miscellaneous	$200
Installation, site preparation, operator training		$4,000
	Initial/Start-up Total Costs:	**$11,170**
Operation cost/year	• Analytical Laboratory Services (effective 1 Oct 02; based on $93/sample[4])	$4,836
	• First Class Shipment Costs (estimated for site to laboratory)	$525
	• Program Coordination	$1,000
	Annual Costs Total:	**$6,361**

First year costs (start-up plus operating costs): $17,531

Subsequent year costs: $6,361

---

[1] Required manufacturers and model: Aerochem Metrics, Inc., 4473 W. Hwy. 476, Bushnell, FL 33513.
Phone: 352/793-8000. Fax;: 352/793-3954 or
LODA Electronics Co., 307 South Elm, PO Box 207, Loda, IL 60948.
Phone: 217/386-2554. Fax:: 217/386-2439. E mail: loelco@net66.com..
Web: www.lodaelectronics.com.

[2] Required manufacturer and model: Option (1) Belfort Instrument Co., 727 S. Wolfe St., Baltimore, MD 21231.
Phone: 410/342-2626. A separate event marker can be purchased from
Aerochem Metrics, Inc. or LODA Electronics Co. ($250) for customer
installation on the Belfort rain gauge.
Option (2) Aerochem Metrics, Inc. offers the required gauge complete with
and event recorder (see footnote 1 for address).

[3] Equipment specifications and suggested models are listed in the *Instruction Manual NADP/NTN Site Operation*

[4] The costs of these agreements are reviewed by the NADP Budget Advisory Committee on an annual basis.

3.0 DATA REPORTING

The following section describes options for reporting wet deposition data, using the Mojave Desert Network as an example. Several data products are produced by the NADP and are available on their website, including national maps and time trends of anions and cations for individual sites, reported in concentration (mg/L) or deposition (kg/ha/yr). Data can also be downloaded from the NADP website and used by NPS Inventory and Monitoring networks for more specific analyses.

3.1 DATA PRODUCTS FROM NADP

The following maps and trend graphs were downloaded directly from the NADP website. On the NADP homepage (http://nadp.sws.uiuc.edu), choose "Isopleth Maps", then "Annual Isopleth Maps". Select a year; maps generally are available by September of the year following collection. There are several maps to choose from; suggested maps include one for nitrogen deposition from nitrate and ammonium ("N Deposition from NO_3 and NH_4") and one for sulfate deposition ("SO_4 Deposition"). Other maps of interest include "NO_3 Concentrations", "NH_4 Concentrations", and "SO_4 Concentrations". Deposition data are useful for evaluating the amount of pollutant that is delivered to an ecosystem; however, deposition is dependent on precipitation amounts (deposition = concentration x precipitation) and may therefore differ significantly from year to year. Concentration data are useful for examining spatial and temporal trends, as concentration is not dependent on precipitation amount.

Nitrate ion concentration, 2003

Sites not pictured:
AK01	0.1 mg/L
AK03	0.2 mg/L
HI99	0.1 mg/L
PR20	0.3 mg/L
VI01	0.3 mg/L

Nitrate as NO_3^- (mg/L)
- ≤ 0.60
- 0.60 - 0.75
- 0.75 - 0.90
- 0.90 - 1.05
- 1.05 - 1.20
- 1.20 - 1.35
- 1.35 - 1.50
- 1.50 - 1.65
- 1.65 - 1.80
- > 1.80

National Atmospheric Deposition Program/National Trends Network
http://nadp.sws.uiuc.edu

Nitrate ion wet deposition, 2003

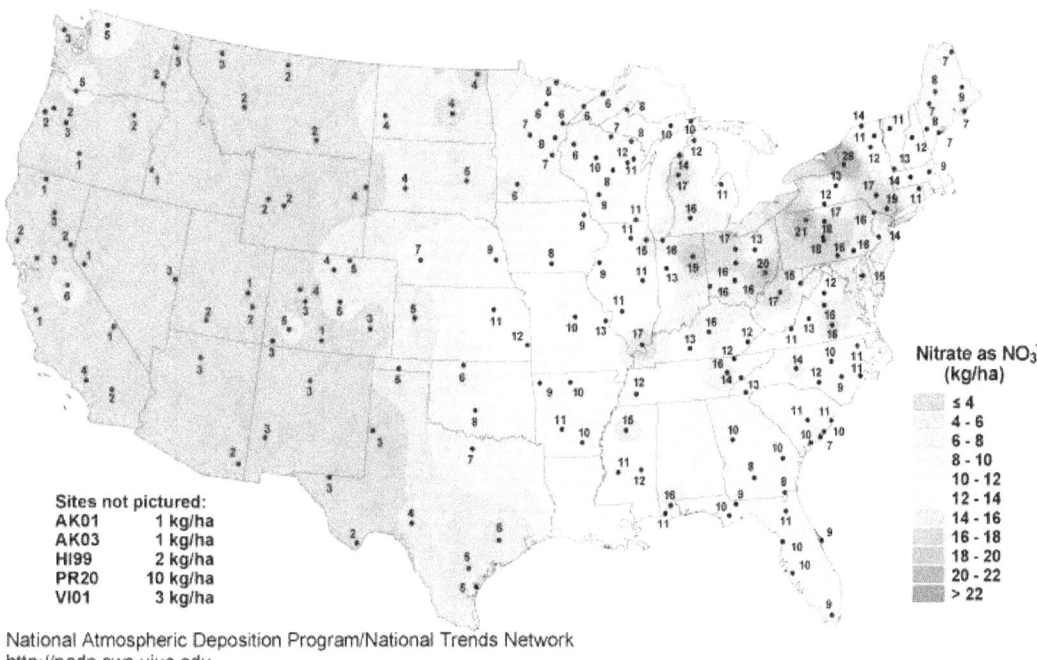

Sites not pictured:
AK01	1 kg/ha
AK03	1 kg/ha
HI99	2 kg/ha
PR20	10 kg/ha
VI01	3 kg/ha

Nitrate as NO_3^- (kg/ha)
- ≤ 4
- 4 - 6
- 6 - 8
- 8 - 10
- 10 - 12
- 12 - 14
- 14 - 16
- 16 - 18
- 18 - 20
- 20 - 22
- > 22

National Atmospheric Deposition Program/National Trends Network
http://nadp.sws.uiuc.edu

Figure 3-1. Spatial distribution of annual precipitation-weighted mean nitrate concentrations and nitrate deposition for 2003 (NADP 2003 Annual Summary from http://nadp.sws.uiuc.edu/).

Sulfate ion concentration, 2003

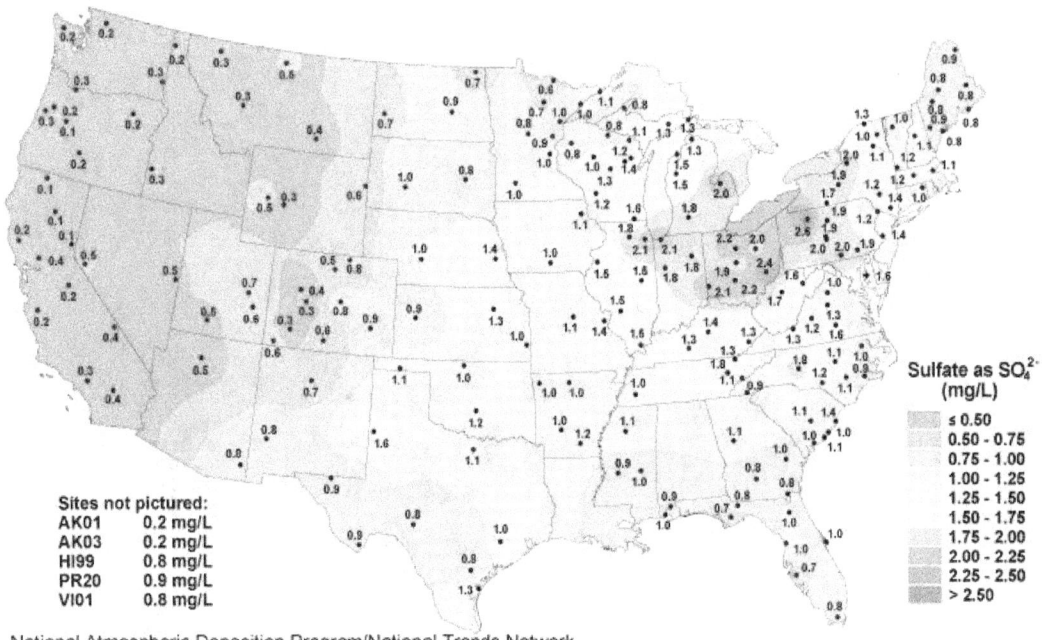

Sites not pictured:
AK01	0.2 mg/L
AK03	0.2 mg/L
HI99	0.8 mg/L
PR20	0.9 mg/L
VI01	0.8 mg/L

Sulfate as SO_4^{2-} (mg/L)

≤ 0.50
0.50 - 0.75
0.75 - 1.00
1.00 - 1.25
1.25 - 1.50
1.50 - 1.75
1.75 - 2.00
2.00 - 2.25
2.25 - 2.50
> 2.50

National Atmospheric Deposition Program/National Trends Network
http://nadp.sws.uiuc.edu

Sulfate ion wet deposition, 2003

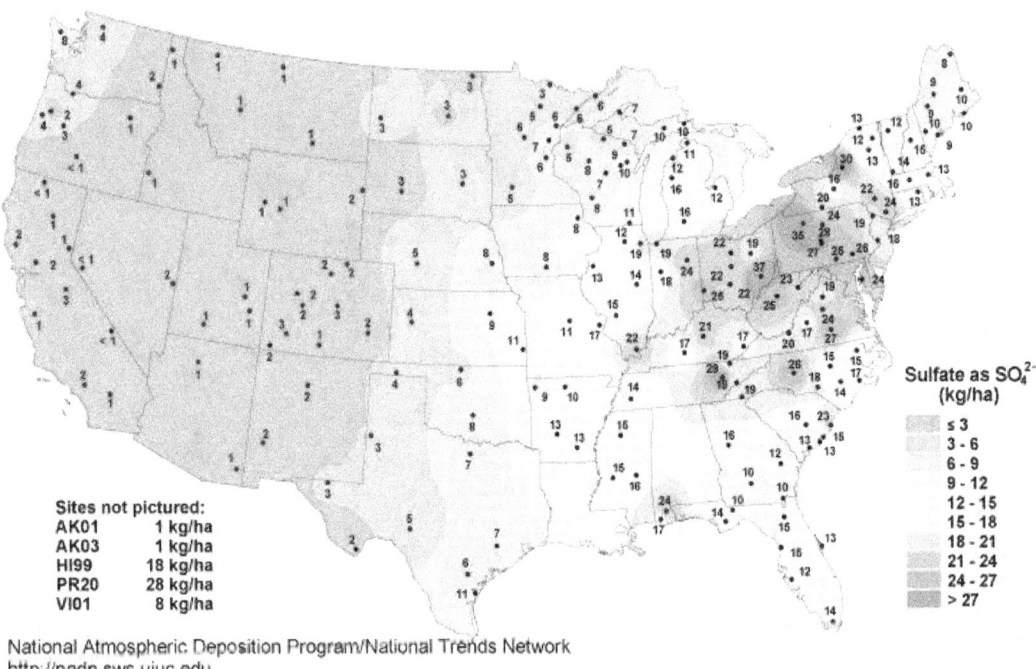

Sites not pictured:
AK01	1 kg/ha
AK03	1 kg/ha
HI99	18 kg/ha
PR20	28 kg/ha
VI01	8 kg/ha

Sulfate as SO_4^{2-} (kg/ha)

≤ 3
3 - 6
6 - 9
9 - 12
12 - 15
15 - 18
18 - 21
21 - 24
24 - 27
> 27

National Atmospheric Deposition Program/National Trends Network
http://nadp.sws.uiuc.edu

Figure 3-2. Spatial distribution of annual precipitation-weighted mean sulfate concentrations and sulfate deposition for 2003 (NADP 2003 Annual Summary from http://nadp.sws.uiuc.edu/).

Networks can use these maps to compare values in their region to values across the country. For example, these maps show that wet deposition of pollutants in the Mojave Desert Network is relatively low when compared to the rest of the country. This is typical of western sites because precipitation is usually much lower in the West than in the East (with the exception of the Pacific Northwest). However, the concentration of nitrate ion is somewhat elevated in portions of the network, possibly indicating influences from the Los Angeles and Las Vegas metro areas (e.g., power plants and autos emit nitrogen oxides, which can transform in the atmosphere to nitrate).

Time trends for individual monitoring locations are also available from the NADP website. For trends at Great Basin NP, on the NADP homepage select "Data Access", click on "Nevada", and select Great Basin NP either from the map or table (site ID is NV05). This page includes site information and provides access to trend plots and annual, monthly, and weekly data (as well as daily data for precipitation). Selecting "Trend Plots" will display a table of the chemical species measured by NADP. A link to "Trends notes" describes how the trend lines were created and discusses data completeness criteria. Data are reported as concentrations (mg/L) or deposition (kg/ha/yr) of pollutants. Concentrations are useful for time trends, as they are not dependent on precipitation amounts. Deposition is useful for evaluating the wet loading of pollutants to the ecosystem. The graphs below show trends in concentrations of NO_3, NH_4, and SO_4 at Great Basin NP from 1985-2003.

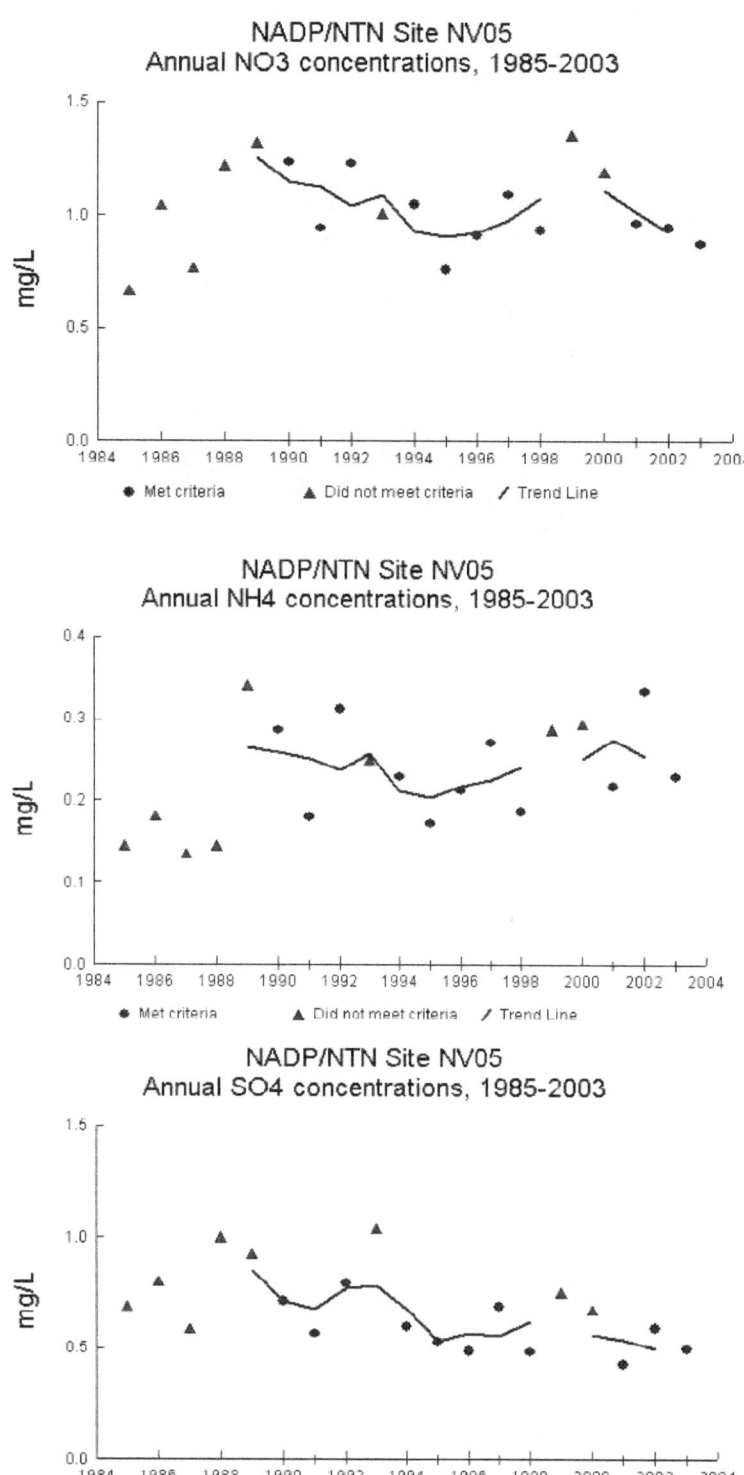

Figure 3-3. Trend lines (composed of a three-year, centered, weighted-moving average value) for wet deposition of nitrate, ammonium, and sulfate at Great Basin NP for 1985-2003 (http://nadp.sws.uiuc.edu/).

At Great Basin NP, NO_3 appears to be decreasing somewhat, NH_4 is remaining steady, and SO_4 is decreasing.

3.2 DATA PRODUCTS FROM ARD

These NADP trend lines represent time series and do not address statistical significance. However, ARD reports trends in air quality parameters every year, with associated statistical significance, in compliance with the Government Performance and Results Act (GPRA) for NPS sites with long-term monitoring. For wet deposition, the parameters are annual sulfate, nitrate, and ammonium concentrations for the past ten years. A nonparametric regression technique (the Theil test), is used to determine statistically significant trends. Probabilities less than or equal to 5 percent are considered to be statistically significant. Increasing or decreasing concentration trends with probabilities less than or equal to 15% are also considered to allow for early detection of deteriorating or improving conditions. Most recent GPRA trends analyses are available at http://www2.nature.nps.gov/air/who/npsPerfMeasures.htm.

ARD is developing additional wet deposition data products, including annual summary charts of concentrations of SO4, NO3, and NH4 in precipitation and wet deposition of nitrogen and sulfur at national parks. Wet deposition of nitrogen and sulfur for 2002 is shown in Figure 3-4. Similar charts for concentrations, and links to other data products are available at http://www2.nature.nps.gov/air/monitoring/wetmon.cfm#data.

2002 Annual Nitrogen Wet Deposition

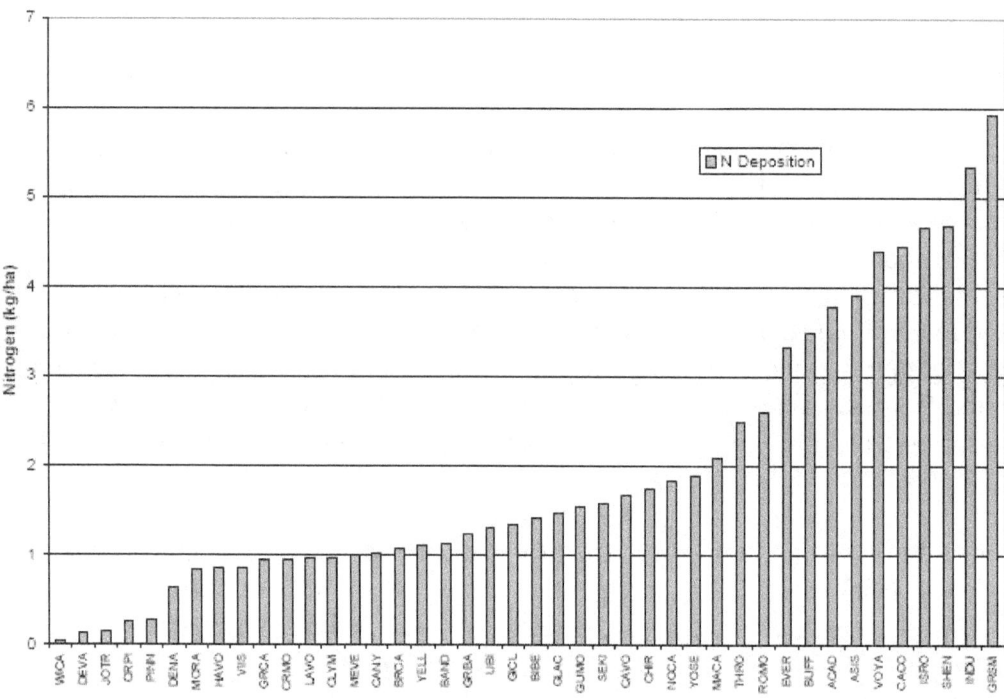

2002 Annual Sulfur Wet Deposition

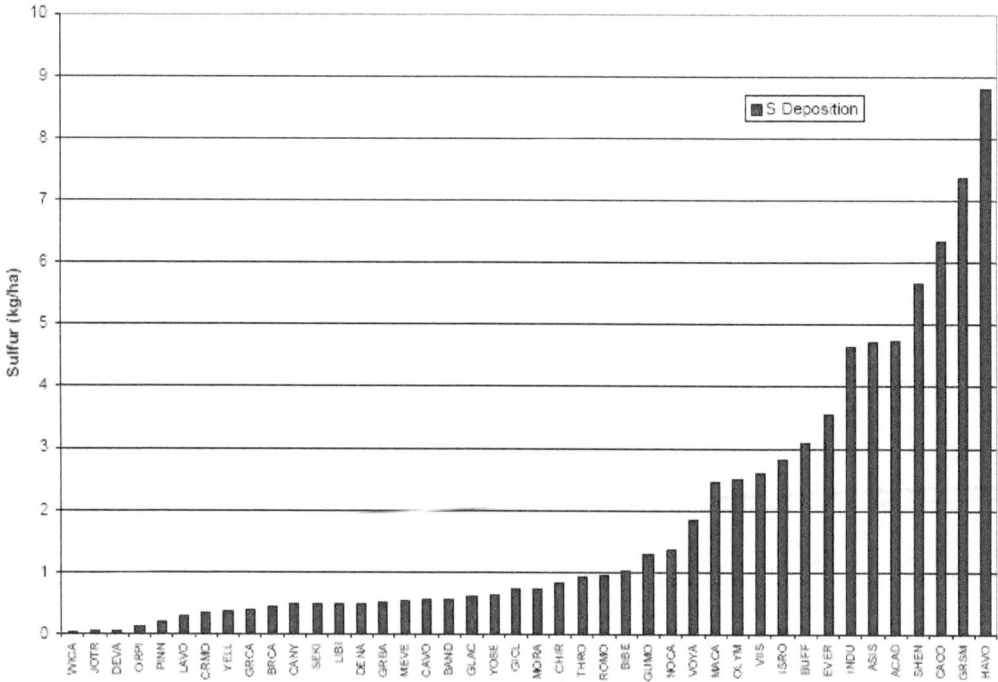

Figure 3-4. Annual summary charts for nitrogen and sulfur wet deposition at NPS sites, 2002 (
http://www2.nature.nps.gov/air/Monitoring/wetmon.cfm#data).

3.3 DATA PRODUCTS FROM CASTNET

CASTNet is the nations' primary monitoring network for estimating dry atmospheric deposition. In addition to providing dry deposition data, CASTNet uses NADP data in conjunction with dry deposition data to report total deposition. From CASTNet's homepage (http://www.epa.gov/castnet/), select "Site Information," then select a site from the map or the site list. Selecting "Joshua Tree NP" (JOT403) will take the user to a site with information about the Joshua Tree NP CASTNet site, as well as a deposition profile that summarizes the composition of total deposition and trends in total deposition for the site. The following pie charts show the contributions of wet and dry chemical species to total deposition in Joshua Tree NP.

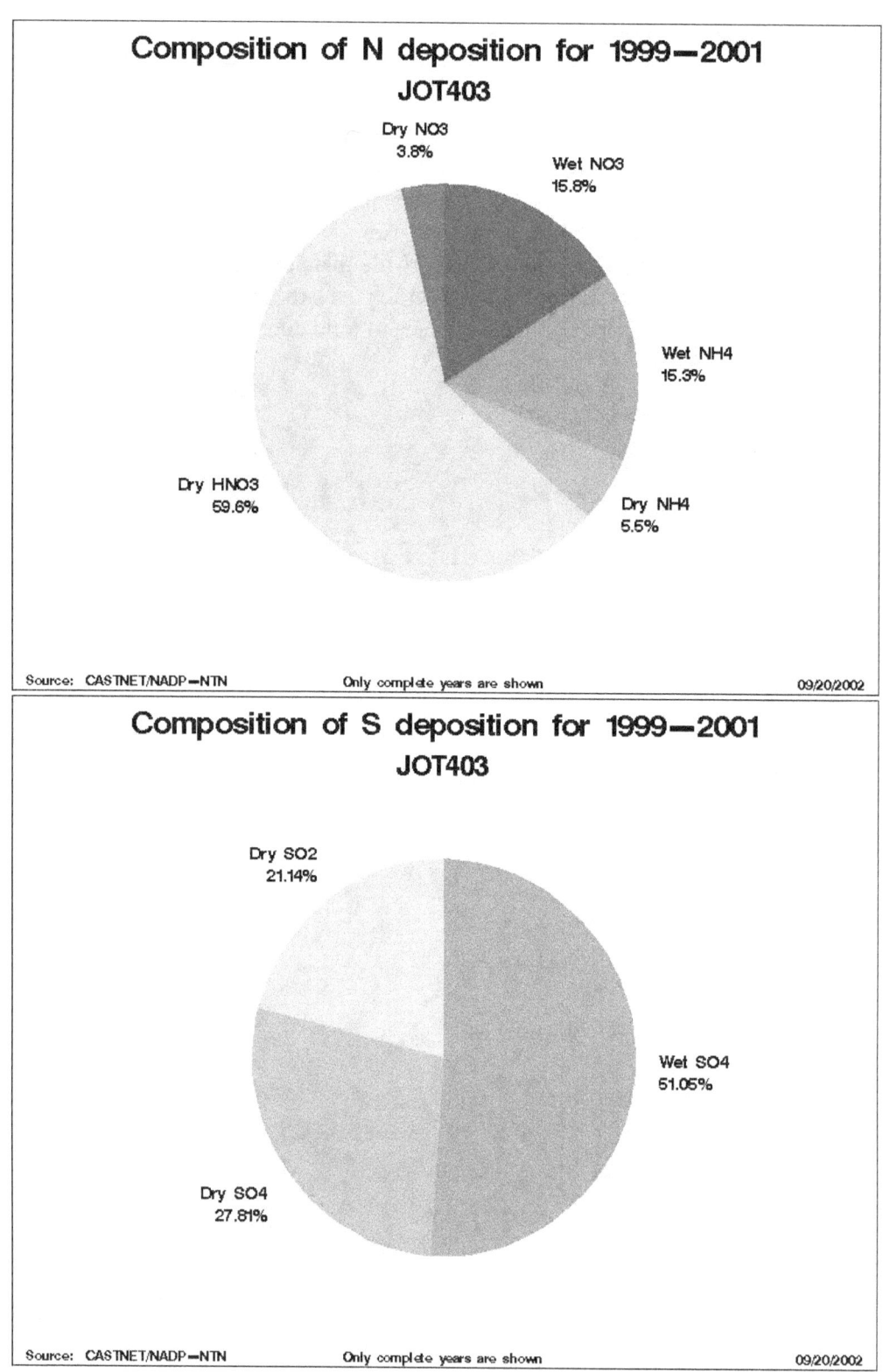

Figure 3-5. Contributions of wet and dry chemical species to total deposition at Joshua Tree NP for 1999-2001 (http://www.epa.gov/castnet/).

Trends in total nitrogen and sulfur deposition at Joshua Tree NP are depicted in the following figure.

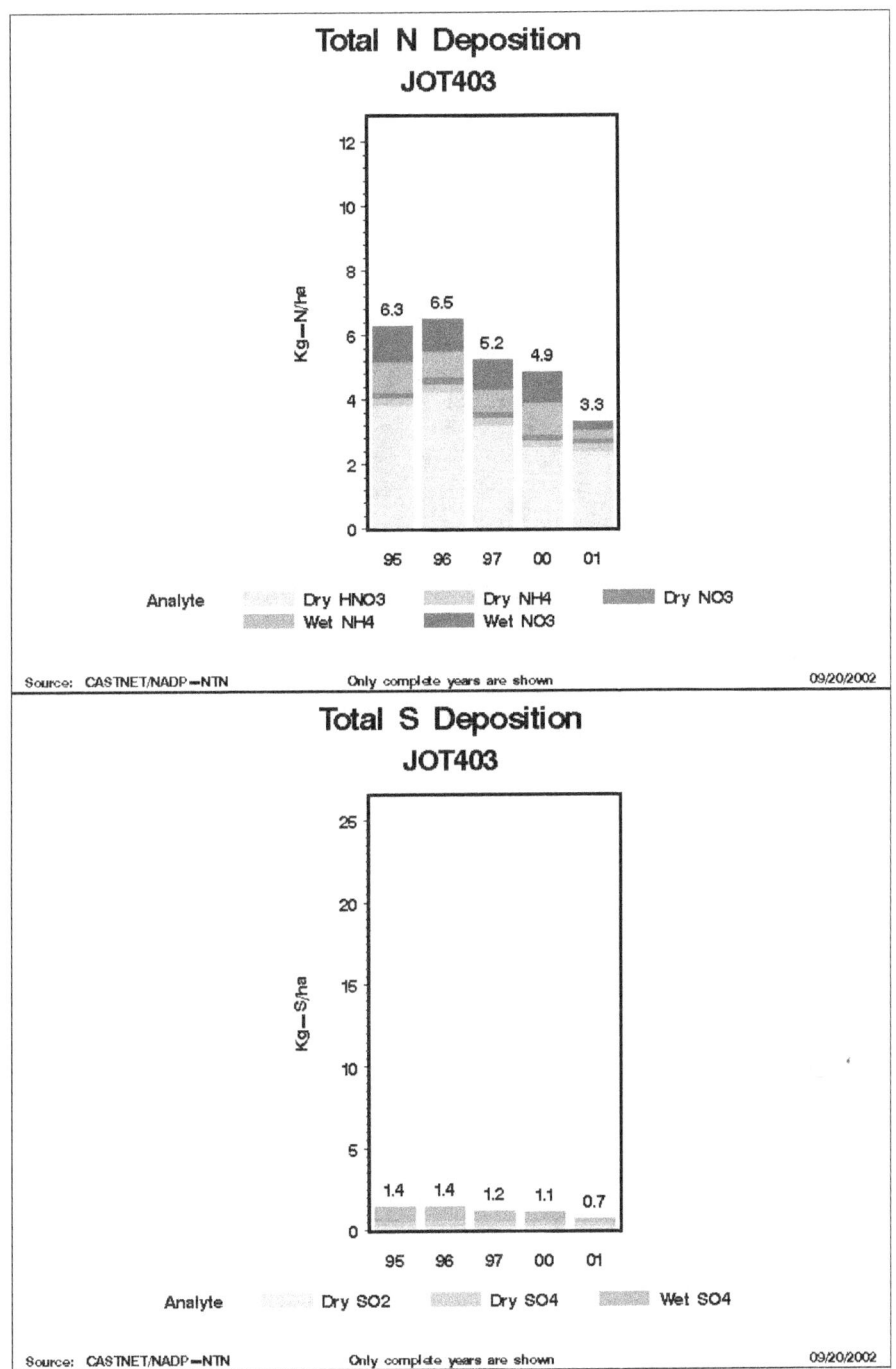

Figure 3-6. Trends in total nitrogen and sulfur deposition at Joshua Tree NP for 1995-2001 (http://www.epa.gov/castnet/).

As described in Section 1-3, natural background deposition for areas in the West has been estimated to be 0.25 kg/ha/yr for either nitrogen or sulfur. Nitrogen deposition is decreasing at Joshua Tree NP, but is still significantly elevated above natural background. There is concern that excess nitrogen is stimulating the growth of exotic weeds and grasses in the park; increases in exotic grasses could increase fire frequency in the park. Research is underway to evaluate the effects of excess nitrogen on the park's ecosystems (study is described at http://www2.nature.nps.gov/air/studies/NSDeposition.htm). Sulfur deposition is low, although above natural background.

3.4 CUSTOM DATA PRODUCTS

In addition to these analyses available on the CASTNet and ARD websites, networks may want to look at concentrations and deposition across their network. Site data for wet deposition can be downloaded from the NADP site by creating a custom site list (example is for Mojave Desert Network):

- NADP homepage (http://nadp.sws.uiuc.edu/)
- "Data Access"
- "Create a customized list for multiple-site data retrievals" (you may have to fill out the data access authorization)
- Use an existing list or scroll to bottom of page and create "List Name" (e.g., Mojave Desert Network) and any other information under "Description"; select "Go"
- Select Joshua Tree, Death Valley, and Great Basin NPs (parks in the Mojave Desert Network that monitor wet deposition)
- Select "Retrieve Data" "Go."
- Select "Annual Data" and fill in the Data Selection Criteria and Intended Use sections; choose water year (Oct-Sept) or calendar year (Jan-Dec)(Note: you will have to download concentration data in mg/L separately from deposition data in kg/ha).
- "Explanatory Notes" at the bottom of the webpage describe NADP's four data completeness criteria and recommended values.

The following two graphs were created in Excel from downloaded data.

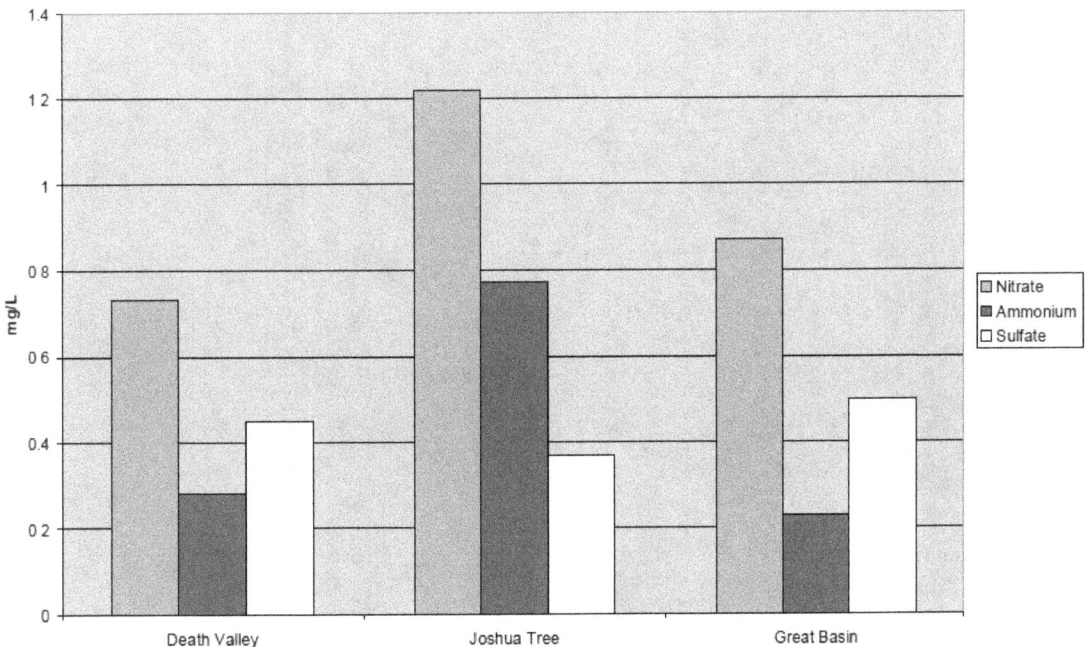

Figure 3-7. Concentrations in milligrams per liter (mg/L) of nitrate, ammonium, and sulfate in wet deposition in three parks in the Mojave Desert Network, 2003 (http://nadp.sws.uiuc.edu/).

In 2003, concentrations of nitrate and ammonium in precipitation were highest at Joshua Tree NP. Sulfate concentrations were generally at Mojave Desert Network sites.

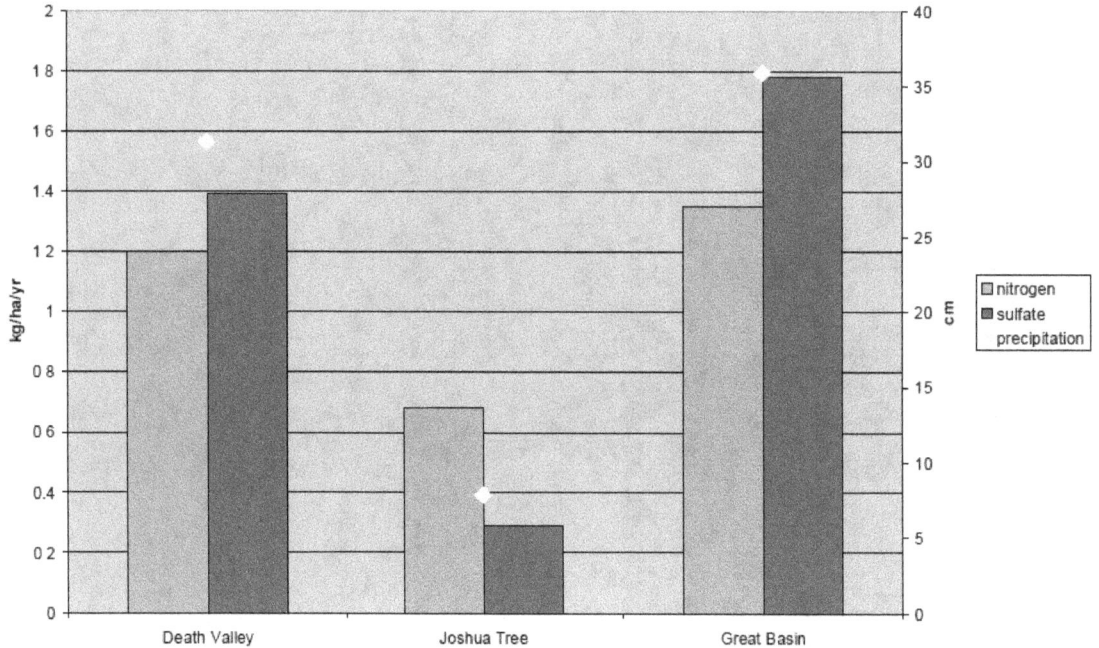

Figure 3-8. Wet deposition in kilograms per hectare per year (kg/ha/yr) of nitrogen and sulfur in 3 parks in the Mojave Desert Network, 2003. Precipitation is shown in centimeters - cm (http://nadp.sws.uiuc.edu/).

In 2003, inorganic nitrogen and sulfate deposition was highest at Great Basin NP. Wet deposition is highly dependent on precipitation amounts; although NO_3 and NH_4 concentrations were highest at Joshua Tree NP, wet deposition was low due to low precipitation amounts.

Because soils and waters are likely to be well-buffered in the area with sufficient levels of base cations, acidification from either nitrate or sulfate is unlikely. However, ecosystems may be sensitive to fertilization by nitrate, with the potential for changes in species composition and abundance.

The NADP publications page (http://nadp.sws.uiuc.edu/lib/) contains additional information on wet deposition data and trends. ARD can also provide guidance on accessing, analyzing, interpreting, and reporting wet deposition data.

The U.S. Department of the Interior (DOI) is the nation's principal conservation agency, charged with the mission "*to protect and provide access to our Nation's natural and cultural heritage and honor our trust responsibilities to Indian tribes and our commitments to island communities.*" More specifically, Interior protects America's treasures for future generations, provides access to our nation's natural and cultural heritage, offers recreation opportunities, honors its trust responsibilities to American Indians and Alaska Natives and its responsibilities to island communities, conducts scientific research, provides wise stewardship of energy and mineral resources, fosters sound use of land and water resources, and conserves and protects fish and wildlife. The work that we do affects the lives of millions of people; from the family taking a vacation in one of our national parks to the children studying in one of our Indian schools.

NPS D-1655, April 2007